The New Orleans Flood Disaster

Written by Nicole Ward

The New Orleans Flood Disaster

Written by Nicole Ward
Cover image of aftermath of Hurricane Katrina
Photography by Reuters/Tranz (p28); Getty Images (Aurora cover; Marko Georgiev p1; David Portnoy p4; Getty Images News p5, p9, p19; James Nielsen p13; Mario Tama p16, p23, p29; David Portnoy p21; Win McNamee p22; Chris Graythen p11, p24)

© 2007 Macmillan Education Australia Pty Ltd

All rights reserved. No part of this publication may be reproduced, stored in a retrieval system, or transmitted in any form or by any means, electronic, mechanical, photocopying, recording, or otherwise, without the prior permission of the copyright owner.

While every care has been taken to trace and acknowledge copyright, the publishers tender their apologies for any accidental infringement where copyright has proved untraceable.

Published by
Macmillan Education Australia Pty Ltd
Level 1, 15–19 Claremont Street, South Yarra, Victoria 3141
www.macmillan.com.au

Edited by Adrian Bell
Designed by Jamie Laurie
Printed in China
25 24 23 22 21 20 19 18 17 16 15 14 13 12 11 10

ISBN: 978-1-4202-6188-2

The New Orleans Flood Disaster

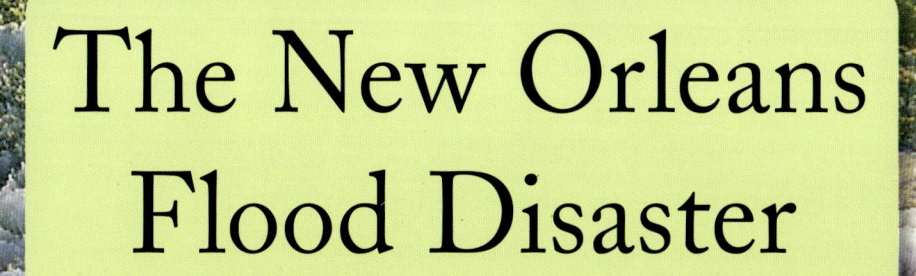

Contents

Introduction 4

Katrina Strikes 8

In the Attic 12

After the Storm 17

The Investigation 25

Glossary 31

Index 32

Introduction

DJ: Welcome to the Radio HJB morning show. Today, we are talking about the horror that Hurricane Katrina caused in New Orleans in August 2005. Elmer Gibson is in the studio with us to share his story. Elmer was in New Orleans when Katrina struck. It caused huge floods and left 80 per cent of the city under water. Elmer witnessed the chaos that left him, and thousands of others, homeless. Katrina took more than 1,600 lives. Five months later, thousands more people are still missing.

The Louisiana Superdome, a refuge for some of the thousands of people who lost their homes

Time line

August 23	August 24	August 25	August 26
Tropical Depression 12 forms near the Bahamas.	Tropical Depression 12 becomes a tropical storm and is renamed Tropical Storm Katrina.		

A view of New Orleans after Hurricane Katrina

DJ: Welcome to the show, Elmer. Can you tell our listeners – when did you first hear about Hurricane Katrina and what did you think about it?

Elmer: I first heard about the hurricane on Thursday, August 25. I was driving home from work when I heard a news report on the radio. It said Katrina had left the sea and moved onto the land, or made **landfall**, in southern Florida. At least five people were already dead. At that stage, the storm was only a category 1 on the scale that measures hurricane strength, the **Saffir-Simpson scale**, so I didn't think much of it. You get used to hearing about hurricanes when you have lived near the Gulf of Mexico all your life.

It wasn't until the next day that I started to pay more attention. I was eating my breakfast when a news report about Katrina came on. The report said it had become much stronger overnight. The scary news was that Katrina seemed to be coming our way. And not only that – it seemed likely that it would be a powerful category 4 hurricane when it touched down. Things were becoming serious. I began to get really worried.

That night, I saw the governor of Louisiana on TV declaring a state of emergency. It sounded as if Hurricane Katrina meant big trouble for New Orleans.

Time line

| August 23 | August 24 | August 25 | August 26 |

August 25 — Katrina becomes a category 1 hurricane and makes landfall in Florida.

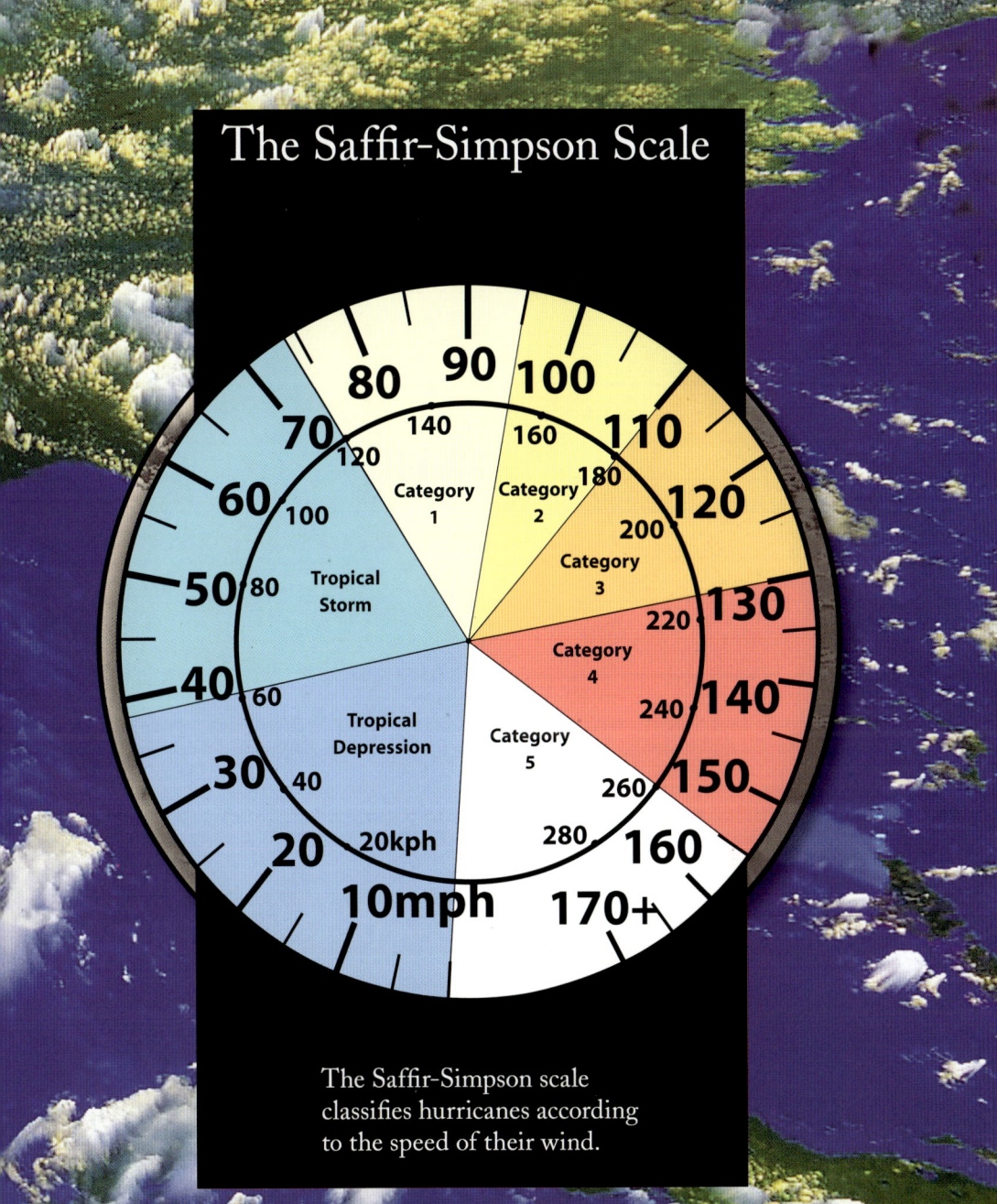

Katrina Strikes

DJ: Why didn't you get out of the city before Hurricane Katrina struck?

Elmer: Believe me, my first thought was to get out of there. I had a bad feeling about Hurricane Katrina and I wanted to get as far away from it as possible. I began planning my escape route in my head. It would take me 40 minutes to load some essential supplies into my van. Then I would go pick up Mum and Dad and we would hit the road. I called my cousin in Houston, Texas, and he offered to let us stay with him until the hurricane had passed.

Unfortunately, my escape plan didn't work out because my parents have lived in New Orleans their entire lives and they didn't want to abandon their home. I told them about the state of emergency, and tried really hard to persuade them that we should escape together. But it was no use; they refused to go. I knew I couldn't leave them there alone, with Hurricane Katrina coming. My parents are in their seventies and I needed to look after them. So I didn't have any choice – I had to stay in New Orleans.

Time line

| August 23 | August 24 | August 25 | August 26 |

Katrina moves into the Gulf of Mexico, becoming a category 2.

By Sunday, August 28, Katrina was very close, and had become a category 5 hurricane. The mayor of New Orleans was on the radio ordering everyone to evacuate the city or go to a shelter. This is called an **evacuation order**. Mum and Dad still refused to go. The three of us watched as people in the neighbourhood packed up and left. The neighbourhood felt like a ghost town. I wasn't surprised when I heard on the radio that nearly a million people were leaving New Orleans. Later, the radio said the roads out of the city were jammed with cars, because of all the people trying to escape. I wished we were escaping with them.

All we could do was sit and wait for Katrina to arrive. We had no idea what was about to hit us.

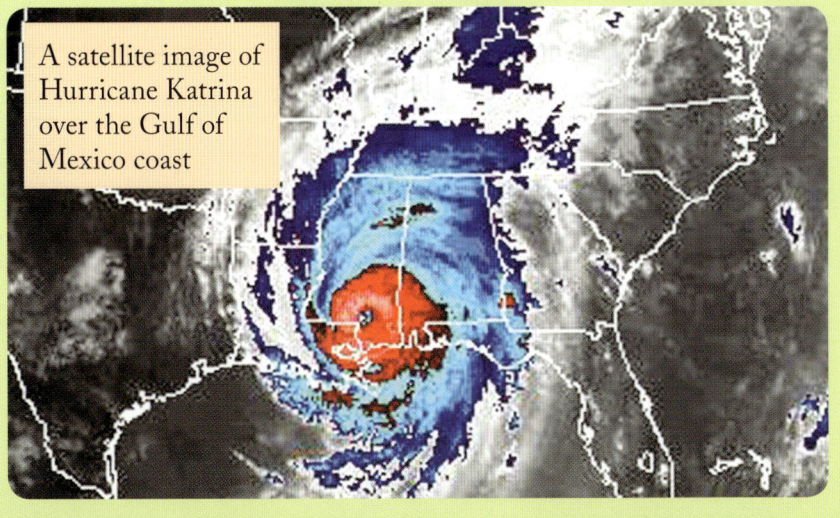

A satellite image of Hurricane Katrina over the Gulf of Mexico coast

Katrina becomes a category 3 and moves west, towards Louisiana.
August 27

Katrina becomes a category 4, then a category 5. The mayor of New Orleans issues an evacuation order.
August 28

August 29

August 30

DJ: When did Hurricane Katrina hit and what happened?

Elmer: We didn't have to wait long for Katrina. It arrived on the morning of Monday, August 29. It had weakened to a category 3 hurricane by then, but it was still powerful. Its winds raged outside the house, ripping street signs from the ground and tearing down power lines.

But it wasn't the savage winds that destroyed my parents' house – it was the floodwater. The hurricane had actually died down a little by mid-morning, and we thought we had come through OK. But then we looked out the window and couldn't believe our eyes. There was a torrent of black water rushing down the street towards the house. The water looked like a big black angry monster swallowing up everything in its way.

I knew we had to get to higher ground, and quickly. We had some life jackets in the basement, and I'd already been down to get them, just in case. I helped my parents into their life jackets and we escaped up into the attic. Soon, the water began pouring into the house, and within 20 minutes it was about 2.5 m deep. The black, polluted water was everywhere and it kept rising. It was hard for Mum and Dad to watch the water destroy their house around them.

Time line

August 23   August 24   August 25   August 26

New Orleans flooded because it is lower than the level of the water around it.

    I couldn't believe there was so much water. I knew New Orleans was vulnerable to flooding because it lies below the natural height of the sea, or **sea level**. But the city had flood barriers, or **levees**, to protect it from flooding – so where was all the water coming from? I wondered if the hurricane had been so violent that it had broken the levees. Or had Katrina caused the sea level to rise up, in a **storm surge**, and send giant waves over the walls that sit on top of the levees? I didn't have the answers. But one thing was certain, the city was flooding.

Katrina weakens to a category 3, and makes landfall again, hitting New Orleans. The levees fail and the city floods.

In the Attic

DJ: What were the conditions in the attic like?

Elmer: It wasn't pleasant in the attic – especially the air up there. It was stinking hot and really humid, as the weather often is after a hurricane. But we did have a good supply of fresh drinking water and food, so we were better off than a lot of others. Still, I would have bought more if I had known how bad things would be. The electricity was out, of course, so at night we would light candles. We passed the time playing cards, but it was a really difficult time for all of us. We were worried about family and friends, but we had no way of contacting them to find out if they were OK.

DJ: Did you know about what was happening outside?

Elmer: On the third day that we were in the attic, a boat came past the house, picking up sick and hurt people and taking them to the Superdome. The people on the boat told us the city was in complete chaos. They also told us that it wasn't a storm surge that had flooded the city – the levees had broken.

Part of a broken levee lies in the floodwaters of New Orleans.

When Katrina struck, the city's main protective levees collapsed and water from nearby Lake Pontchartrain poured into the city. New Orleans is bowl-shaped, and when the city flooded the bowl filled up. The people in the boat told us that most of New Orleans was flooded and some neighbourhoods were under as much as 6 m of water. The worst affected were those people living in the low-lying areas. I was sad to hear that most of these people were the poorer inhabitants of New Orleans. It didn't seem fair. As the city flooded, a lot of them had to swim for their lives. The floodwaters completely washed their homes away.

People begin to flee to the Superdome to escape the floodwaters.

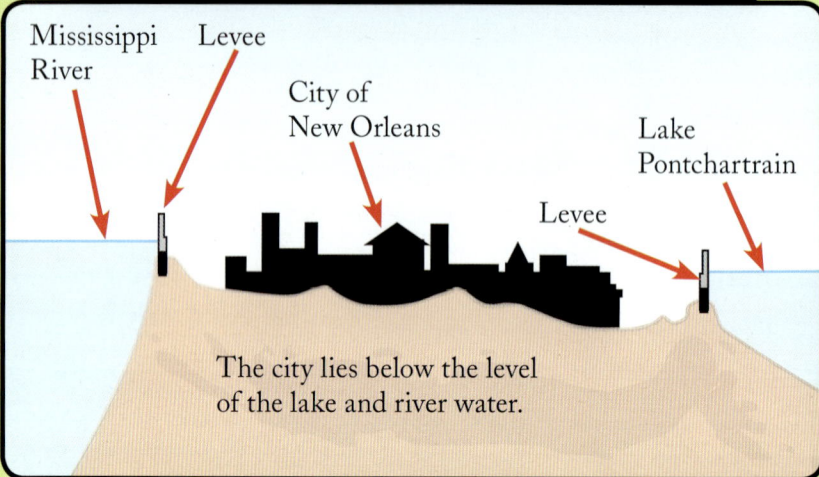

Cross-Section of New Orleans

The city lies below the level of the lake and river water.

All across the city, there was no power, no drinking water, and very little food. One of the people on the boat told us there were people stealing from empty shops, or **looting**, in the city. Looters were throwing rocks through store windows and taking off with stuff. He said many of the people looting the stores were not hardened criminals. They were desperate, and were stealing fresh water and food to feed their families.

Shopkeepers were left to defend their own property. We heard the story of one shopkeeper who opened his doors and said: "Take whatever you want, just don't wreck the store." He lost all his goods, but he prevented the looters from ruining his store.

Time line

August 24   August 25   August 26   August 27

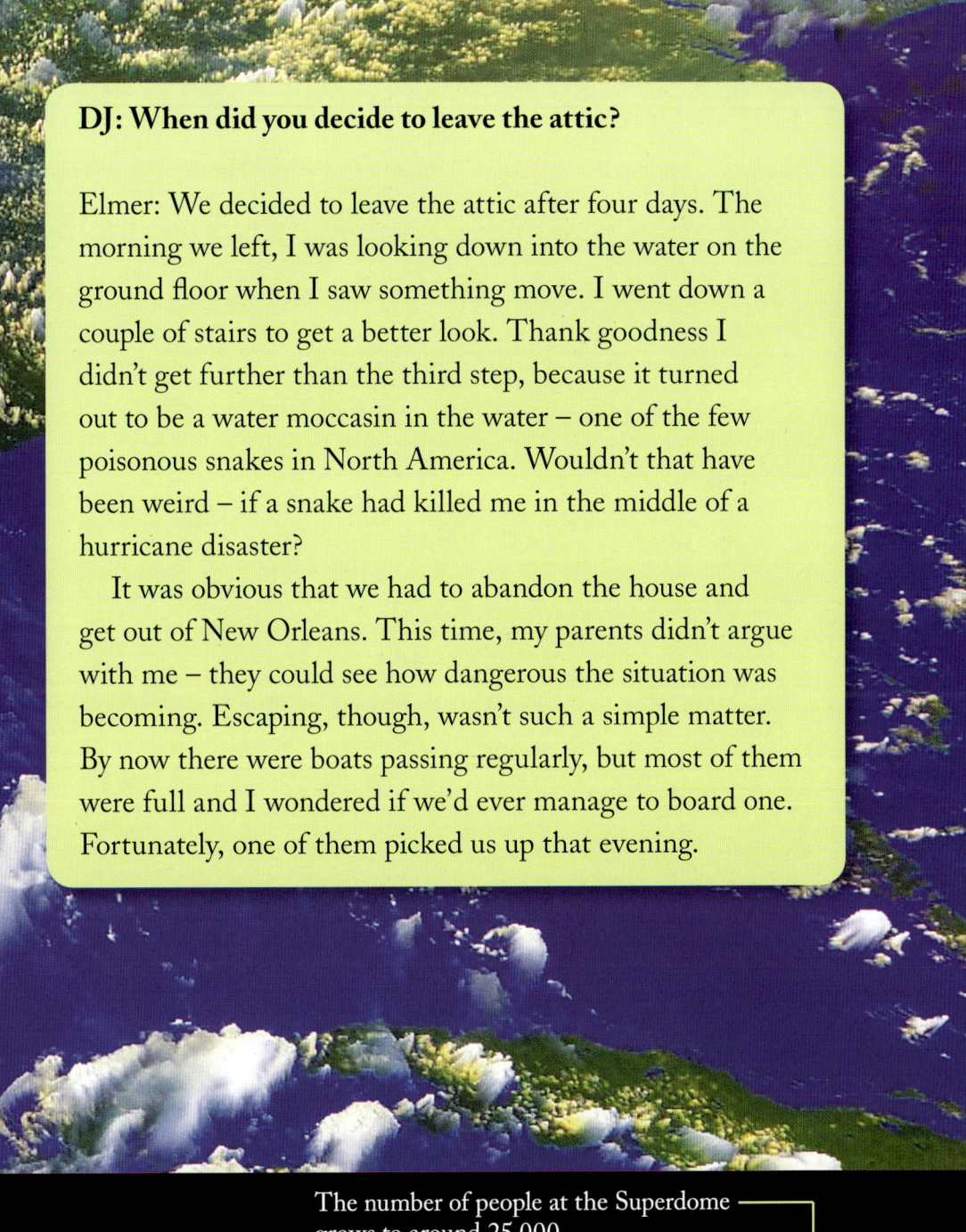

DJ: When did you decide to leave the attic?

Elmer: We decided to leave the attic after four days. The morning we left, I was looking down into the water on the ground floor when I saw something move. I went down a couple of stairs to get a better look. Thank goodness I didn't get further than the third step, because it turned out to be a water moccasin in the water – one of the few poisonous snakes in North America. Wouldn't that have been weird – if a snake had killed me in the middle of a hurricane disaster?

It was obvious that we had to abandon the house and get out of New Orleans. This time, my parents didn't argue with me – they could see how dangerous the situation was becoming. Escaping, though, wasn't such a simple matter. By now there were boats passing regularly, but most of them were full and I wondered if we'd ever manage to board one. Fortunately, one of them picked us up that evening.

The number of people at the Superdome grows to around 25,000.

My poor parents were crying – they understood that they would never see their home again. We took hardly anything with us on the boat – just some clothing and the last remaining food and fresh water.

The dirty, polluted water surrounded the boat. I remember the bubbles of gas everywhere I looked. The water was like a toxic soup, filled with sewage, chemicals, rubbish, and even dead animals, and it smelled so awful. I will never forget the terrible smell of that water.

People had to leave their homes and try to escape with whatever they could carry.

We were lucky that the three of us were still together. One of the people in our boat didn't know if his family was dead or alive. He had been at work when Hurricane Katrina struck, and had no idea if his wife and six-month-old son had survived.

After the Storm

DJ: Did you consider taking your parents to the Superdome to escape the floodwater?

Elmer: The man on the boat told us we shouldn't go to the Superdome. It was supposed to be a safe place with food and water, a **refuge**, but the authorities hadn't planned it properly. It was overcrowded, the toilets were overflowing, and it was stinking hot. There was no air conditioning and the temperature was in the high thirties, so the people inside were baking hot. There were almost no supplies of food or water, and people went for days without eating. There was a lot of violence and theft there, too. A friend of mine stayed in the Superdome and he almost never slept because people would try to steal his stuff and go through his pockets. He had to keep one eye open the whole time.

The first busloads of refugees from the Superdome arrive in Houston.

August 29 | August 30 | August 31 | September 1

DJ: Can you describe what you saw when you were travelling around on the boat?

Elmer: There were people all around us in the water. Many people had squashed themselves into boats or canoes, and some were even on makeshift rafts. Everything that could float was on the water, packed with people and their pets trying to escape. Some people were wading through the streets with the dirty water up to their waists. I remember thinking how much disease there must be in that water.

The devastation around us was incredible, an entire city under water. The New Orleans I grew up in seemed to have disappeared, and there was this strange, dangerous nightmare in its place. We could hear gunfire off in the distance. People told us there was a lot of crime going on in the city – not just looting, but violent fights and carjacking as well. There weren't enough police to control the crime breaking out all over New Orleans.

Time line

| August 26 | August 27 | August 28 | August 29 |

We went past a shop with a spray-painted sign saying: "You Loot, I Shoot." The shopkeeper was sitting on the roof of his shop with his gun and he looked as if he meant business. With the city being in so much chaos, everyone had to look out for themselves, I suppose. A lot of people had climbed onto their rooftops to escape the water. We saw helicopters circling in the air rescuing stranded people. It looked as if the United States Coast Guard was rescuing people with the help of navy and army helicopters.

A Coast Guard helicopter rescues two children from a rooftop.

Texas officials say that there are around 154,000 refugees from New Orleans in Texas.

August 30   August 31   September 1   September 2

DJ: Where did your boat take you?

Elmer: The boat took us to the Mississippi levee. Our plan was to get on the Chalmette ferry and over to a staging area where we could catch the bus to my cousin's place in Houston. I wanted to get my parents far away from New Orleans. It had become a dangerous and disease-ridden city.

We arrived at the Mississippi levee and my heart sank when I saw that there were hundreds of people waiting for the ferry. We were going to be waiting for hours, perhaps days. But we had no alternative – what else could we do?

There were a handful of coast guards trying to control the crowds, but they were getting nowhere. People were pushing and shoving, trying to get ahead in the queue. Ferries arrived and departed, and still we waited in that terrible heat. I was getting worried about my parents, who were exhausted – I didn't know how much more they could take. Hours and hours passed, and finally they allowed us onto the ferry. People crowded onto it like sardines, packed so close you couldn't move a muscle. It was horrible, but at least the waiting was over.

Time line

| August 27 | August 28 | August 29 | August 30 |

It was raining when the ferry arrived at the staging area, which just added to the misery. The ferry terminal had been awful, but the staging area was even worse. There were thousands of desperate, angry people waiting for buses. They were exhausted and hungry, and angry at having to wait days for a bus. And they were angry, too, that they had lost everything in the floodwaters. You could see it all on their faces.

A lot of buses went straight past us because they were full. We waited over 20 hours, getting more and more frustrated. When we eventually boarded a bus, it wasn't going to Texas, where my cousin lives. But we didn't care – we just wanted to get away from the staging area, and away from New Orleans.

Refugees in Houston wait for their relatives to arrive from New Orleans.

The last 300 people leave the Superdome.

August 31   September 1   September 2   September 3

DJ: What do you feel when you look back on what happened?

Elmer: It was a terrible tragedy, and a waste of so many lives, more than a thousand people. So many of the people who did survive lost everything they owned. I feel saddened when I remember how people suffered. And sometimes I feel angry when I wonder if the authorities could have done more, before the hurricane and after it. Could the levees have been better built? Could the rescue operation have been better organized? Where were the supplies of food and fresh water? I could carry on asking questions but it's just going to frustrate me and get me nowhere.

A bell from a church that Katrina destroyed

Time line

August 28   August 29   August 30   August 31

What does make me feel good, and what most people haven't heard about, is stories of the real heroes of the hurricane rescue. People who saved strangers. Neighbours who saved neighbours still trapped in their houses. People who swam in the dirty water to rescue the old and the sick. Nurses who kept unconscious patients alive. A lot of these people had lost their homes and had not heard from their families yet they stayed and looked after other people. The community spirit shown by these people is the only good thing that came out of this tragedy.

A man braves the floodwaters to bring drinking water to his neighbours.

Search-and-rescue helicopters continue to save people trapped on roofs and in attics.

September 1   September 2   September 3   September 4

DJ: We cannot even begin to understand what you have been through. I'd like to extend our sympathies to you, and to all the people of New Orleans. Thank you for coming and sharing your story of survival.

As well as the loss of life, Katrina did terrible damage to buildings in New Orleans.

Time line

| August 29 | August 30 | August 31 | September 1 |

The Investigation

DJ: Welcome back, everyone. We're still talking about Hurricane Katrina. Joining us is disaster management expert, Dr Erica Swift. Dr Swift, tell us – what went wrong in New Orleans?

Dr Swift: Plenty of things went wrong, but the key was lack of preparation. You see, nothing that happened was unexpected. People have always known that New Orleans was at risk. A government report after the flood said, "Katrina was not just predictable. It was predicted." In 2004, Louisiana emergency agencies held a practice exercise. They wanted to study what would happen if a large storm hit New Orleans. It was called the Hurricane Pam exercise. The results were very close to what happened the next year, when the real hurricane struck.

The United States Army starts pumping water out of New Orleans.

September 2 | September 3 | September 4 | September 5

DJ: What do you mean, people have "always known" that New Orleans was at risk?

Dr Swift: The first settlers who came to New Orleans knew that they were building in a dangerous place. Most of the land used to be swamp. It now consists of soft silt, sand, and clay, which naturally sink. New Orleans has been sinking about a metre each century since it was built.

People have also always known the risk of building a city below sea level. It is especially risky to have a large body of water on either side that is higher than the city itself. It's always been obvious that if the levees failed, water from Lake Pontchartrain and the Mississippi River would flood the city.

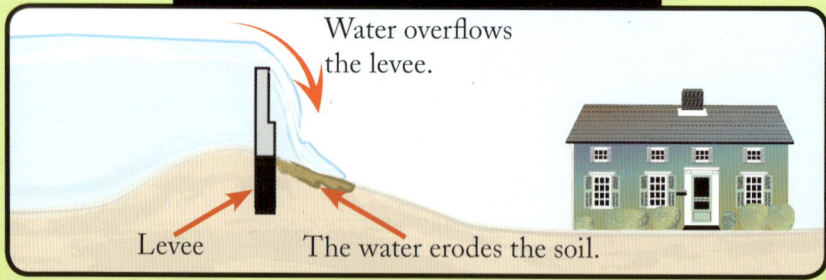

Failure of the Levees

DJ: But did people know that the levees might fail?

Dr Swift: Over the years, many experts have said that the levees would not be strong enough if a really big hurricane hit the city. After Katrina, a New Orleans newspaper headline said, "Katrina: The Storm We've Always Feared." That's absolutely right. Scientists had often said that a storm like Katrina would flood the city.

Dr Joe Suhayda is a water resources expert. He also predicted what would happen. He said that a category 4 hurricane would put the city under 6 m of water. He also talked about the sewage plants in the city and the chemical plants on the Mississippi River. He said that if they flooded, they would turn the water into a deadly brew. When Katrina struck, all of what he said came true.

Experts also predicted the refugee problem. In the Hurricane Pam exercise, they said a million people would have to flee. They also said that thousands of people would not get out in time. As we saw, however, the city was not prepared for that problem either.

DJ: Why did it take so long to help the people who stayed behind?

Dr Swift: The first problem was that they were still there at all. When they knew how bad Katrina was going to be, the city authorities gave an evacuation order. But there were more than 100,000 people who weren't able to leave. They are poor, and don't have cars, or enough money to pay for transport and shelter outside the city.

Refugees in New Orleans walk past the Superdome.

The authorities set up 12 locations where people could go to catch buses. The buses would take them to the Superdome. But the Superdome was supposed to be a "refuge of last resort." People were only supposed to go there if they absolutely couldn't stay in their homes. The authorities didn't think very many people would have to go there. So they didn't prepare enough food, water, medicine, and transport.

Of course, after the levees broke, thousands and thousands of people absolutely had to leave their homes, because the homes were under water. They had to go to the refuge of last resort. When they got there, the Superdome wasn't ready to handle them.

The Superdome was an inadequate refuge for people who escaped the flood.

DJ: What lessons do you think we should learn from what happened to New Orleans?

Dr Swift: I think the lesson is a very simple one; we just have to remember it. Always be prepared. There were no surprises about Hurricane Katrina – experts and scientists knew what had to be done. The problem is that it wasn't done. We need to do everything possible to prevent disasters like the failure of the levees, and we need to have plans ready if the disaster does actually come. One government official in New Orleans said that everyone knew what they would need when the hurricane hit, but it wasn't until after it hit that they started looking for these things. He said "The system needed to go into automatic." If we have a plan that goes into automatic next time, then we'll be able to take what a hurricane like Katrina throws at us.

DJ: Well, let's hope we are prepared next time. I think that's the best tribute we could ever pay to the people who died in New Orleans. Dr Swift, thank you for your time.

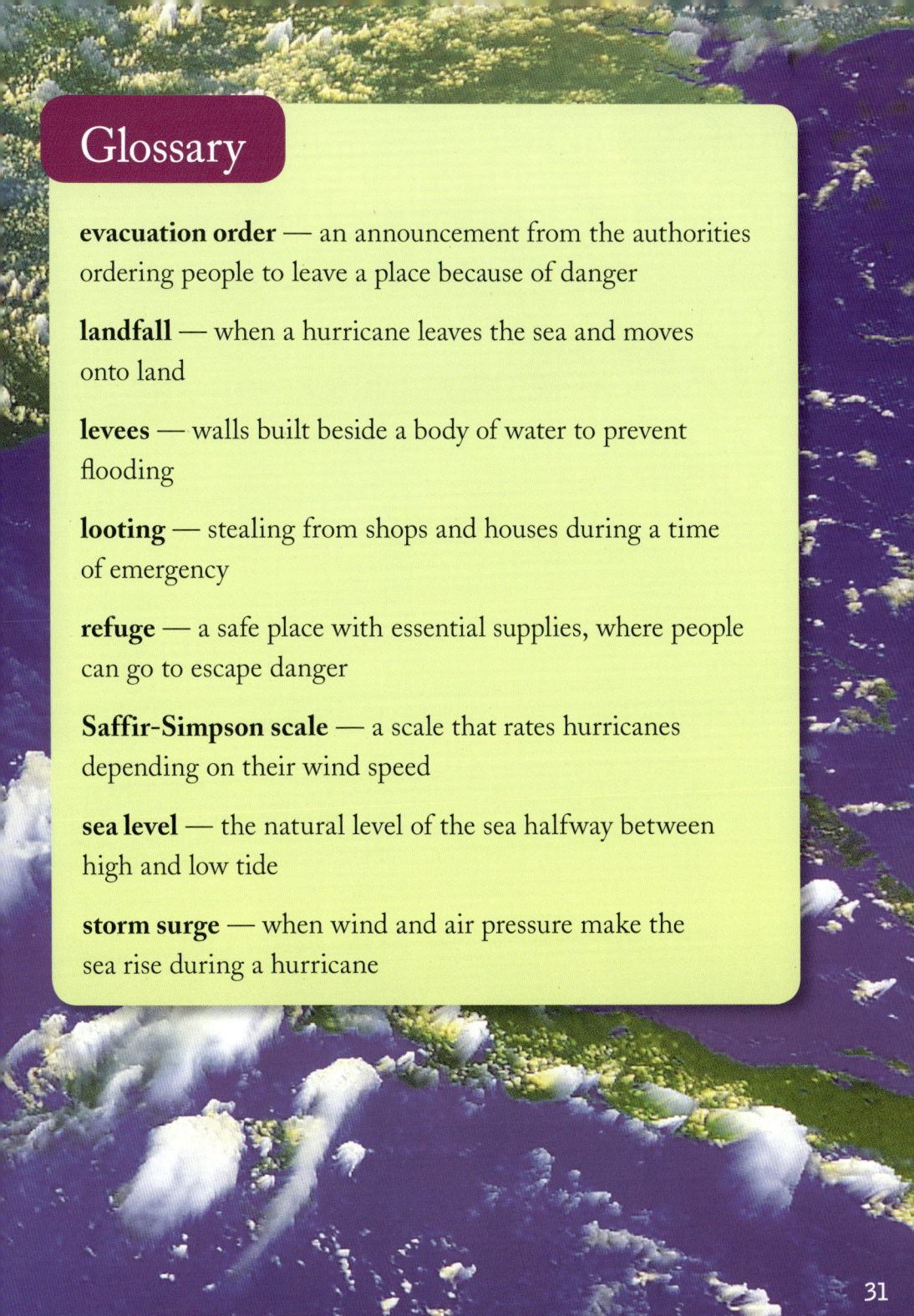

Glossary

evacuation order — an announcement from the authorities ordering people to leave a place because of danger

landfall — when a hurricane leaves the sea and moves onto land

levees — walls built beside a body of water to prevent flooding

looting — stealing from shops and houses during a time of emergency

refuge — a safe place with essential supplies, where people can go to escape danger

Saffir-Simpson scale — a scale that rates hurricanes depending on their wind speed

sea level — the natural level of the sea halfway between high and low tide

storm surge — when wind and air pressure make the sea rise during a hurricane

Index

boat(s) 12–18, 20

bus(es) 20, 21, 29

evacuation order 9, 28

Lake Pontchartrain 13, 14, 26

levee(s) 11–14, 20, 22, 26, 27, 29, 30

looting 14, 18

Mississippi River 14, 26, 27

refugee(s) 17, 19, 21, 27, 28

storm surge 11, 12

Superdome 4, 12, 13, 15, 17, 21, 28, 29